HOW TO BE A GREAT MANAGER

Master the Art of Leadership

Ray Goodwin

CONTENTS

LIABILITY DISCLAIMER

damages, or losses that may arise from their use of the information contained herein.

CHAPTER 1: INTRODUCTION TO MANAGEMENT

Managing people can be one of the most rewarding experiences you ever undertake in your career, but it can also be one of the most challenging. Whether you're leading a small team or overseeing an entire department, being a great manager requires a unique set of skills and qualities that go beyond just technical expertise.

In this book, I will share with you my 25 years of experience managing teams and individuals across various industries. I will walk you through the key principles of effective management and provide you with practical tips and strategies to help improve your leadership skills.

The book is for both new and experienced managers who are looking to enhance their knowledge and learn how to develop successful relationships with their employees. From delegation to communication, motivation to conflict resolution, each chapter covers a different aspect of management that will help you become an effective leader in any workplace.

So whether you're just starting out as a manager or looking to take your leadership skills to the next level, How To Be A Great Manager has everything you need to succeed. So let's get started on this exciting journey towards becoming the best manager you can be!

Let's Begin

Management is a practice that has been around for centuries, yet it is still one of the most significant and influential aspects of the modern business world. In essence, management is the art of getting things done through people. Managers are responsible for overseeing people, processes, and resources to achieve organizational goals effectively. The importance of effective management cannot be overemphasized; it determines the success or failure of a business. Therefore, it is necessary for aspiring managers to understand the various types of managers, their roles and responsibilities, the skills they need, the common challenges they face and what it takes to become a great manager.

Definition of management

Management is the coordination and control of activities to achieve organizational goals. It involves planning, organizing, staffing, directing, and controlling resources to accomplish the set objectives. Fundamentally, management is the process of creating, operating, and continuously improving a system that can produce the desired outcomes. A good manager must also be able to lead and motivate their team while ensuring that they work within ethical boundaries.

Importance of effective management

Effective management is vital to the success of any organization. Managers are responsible for making sure that employees work together efficiently and meet the company's goals and objectives. A successful manager must also be able to build a culture of trust and accountability, where employees feel valued and empowered to contribute to the organization's success. A poorly managed team can result in low morale, high employee turnover, poor-quality work, and waste of resources.

Different types of managers

There are various types of managers, each with a different specialization and focus. Some of the common types of managers include:

- ❖ General Manager – Responsible for the overall success of an organization.

- ❖ Departmental Manager – Heads a particular department or area of the organization.

- ❖ Project Manager – Oversees specific projects from start to finish.

- ❖ Operations Manager – Manages day-to-day operations in an organization.

- ❖ Human Resource Manager – Responsible for staffing, training, and development of employees.

- ❖ Financial Manager - Manages the organization's financial resources.

Roles and responsibilities of managers

The roles and responsibilities of managers vary depending on their area of specialization, but some common responsibilities include:

- ➢ Planning – Developing goals, objectives, and policies to achieve company success.

- ➢ Organizing – Assigning responsibilities, delegating tasks and resources.

- ➢ Staffing – Hiring the right people, providing training, and career development opportunities.

- ➢ Directing – Guiding and motivating employees to achieve

organizational goals.

➢ Controlling – Monitoring performance, identifying and correcting problems, and ensuring that the company's goals are met.

Skills required to become a great manager

Becoming a great manager is not only about technical expertise but also requires soft skills and emotional intelligence. Some of the essential skills required to become a great manager include:

❖ Strong communication skills that can convey a clear message to employees.

❖ Empathy - The ability to understand and relate to people's emotions, helping managers make better decisions and build more productive teams.

❖ Leadership skills – Setting expectations, inspiring, mentoring, and coaching employees to achieve their goals.

❖ Critical thinking and problem-solving - The ability to identify problems and think critically to come up with solutions.

❖ Time management - The ability to prioritize and manage time effectively to meet organizational goals.

❖ Adaptability - The ability to respond to change and embrace innovation.

❖ Collaboration - The ability to work with and coordinate with people from different departments or backgrounds.

Common challenges faced by managers

Effective management is not easy, and managers face various challenges every day. Some of these challenges include:

❖   Managing a diverse workforce with different skill sets or backgrounds.

❖   Resolving conflicts between employees.

❖   Dealing with difficult customers or clients.

❖   Implementing organization-wide changes.

❖   Managing employee performance and keeping them motivated.

❖   Managing finances and budgets.

Overview of the book

This book aims to equip managers and aspiring managers with the tools necessary to be successful in their roles. It covers a broad range of topics, including understanding organizational structure and culture, communication skills, building and leading teams, managing change, setting goals and objectives, managing time, problem-solving and decision-making, performance management, motivating employees, negotiation skills, ethical and legal considerations, managing diversity, managing performance and stress, financial management, leadership development, networking and professional development, managing remote teams, crisis management, and taking action.

What readers can expect to learn

In this book, readers will discover how to become great managers who can create a positive work environment where employees are motivated, engaged, and accountable. They will learn how to effectively manage teams, communicate, negotiate, make decisions, adapt to change, set goals, and manage performance. They will also discover how to manage diversity, build resilience, and lead with integrity. At the end of each chapter, readers will find practical tips and exercises that they can use to apply the lessons learned. By the end of the book, readers will have the knowledge, skills, and confidence to excel as managers and drive their team's success.

CHAPTER 2: UNDERSTANDING THE ORGANIZATION

As a manager, one of the first things you must do is understand the organization you work for. This means understanding its structure, culture, goals, values, stakeholders, and relationships. Only by understanding these factors can you effectively manage your team and contribute to the success of the organization. In this chapter, we will explore these aspects of the organization in more detail.

Overview of Organizational Structure

Every organization has a structure – a way of organizing tasks, people, and resources. Understanding this structure is vital for any manager. The organizational structure defines how different departments and teams are structured, who reports to whom, and who is responsible for what. It also outlines how information flows within the organization.

For example, in a hierarchical organization, there will be a clear chain of command, with each employee reporting to a single supervisor. In a matrix organization, there may be several layers of management and a more complex reporting structure. Regardless of the type of organizational structure, as a manager, it's important to understand the structure and your role within it.

Importance of Understanding the Company Culture

The company culture is the shared values, beliefs, norms, and practices that shape the behavior of employees within the organization. It defines what is acceptable and what is not. Understanding the company culture is important because it gives you insight into the organization's values, mission, and purpose. This information can help you align your team's goals and priorities with those of the organization.

It's also important to understand the company culture because it affects employee motivation and engagement. If a manager creates a work environment that aligns with the company culture, employees are more likely to feel valued, respected, and engaged. In contrast, if a manager ignores or contradicts the company culture, employees may feel disengaged and unmotivated.

Identifying the Company's Goals and Objectives

The organization's goals and objectives are the targets it aims to achieve. These targets should be specific, measurable, achievable, relevant, and time-bound (SMART). As a manager, you should align your team's goals with those of the organization to ensure that everyone is working towards the same end.

Understanding the company's goals and objectives also helps you prioritize tasks and allocate resources effectively. It enables you to identify the key performance indicators (KPIs) that are essential to measuring progress and success. In short, understanding the company's goals and objectives is the foundation for effective management.

Understanding the Company's History and Values

The history and values of an organization can provide insight into its mission, culture, and strengths. For example, a company that has been in business for decades will have a different history and culture than a startup. Similarly, an organization with a focus on social responsibility will operate differently than one that prioritizes profit above all else.

As a manager, understanding the company's history and values can help you make decisions that align with the organization's culture and values. It can also help you communicate more effectively with employees, stakeholders, and customers.

Understanding the Company's Stakeholders

Stakeholders are individuals or groups who have an interest in the organization's operations, success, or failure. These may include employees, customers, investors, partners, competitors, government agencies, and the community at large.

Understanding the stakeholders of the organization is important for several reasons. It helps you understand the needs and expectations of different groups and how they impact the organization's operations. It also helps you prioritize stakeholders based on their level of importance and influence. And finally, it enables you to build relationships with key stakeholders that are critical to the organization's success.

Building Relationships with Colleagues Across Departments

No manager can be an island. Building relationships with colleagues across departments is essential for success. These relationships can help you identify opportunities, solve problems, and collaborate on projects. They can also provide support and insight when you need it most.

Networking with colleagues across departments can also help you develop your leadership skills. You can learn from the experiences of others, keep up-to-date on trends and best practices, and build your professional reputation.

Building Alliances with Key Players in the Organization

In addition to colleagues across departments, building alliances with key players in the organization is critical for success. These individuals may include executives, board members, influential employees, and stakeholders.

Building alliances with key players can help you gain valuable support and resources for your team. It can also give you a voice in important decisions and help you navigate the political landscape of the organization.

Maintaining a Positive Image of Yourself and the Team

Finally, as a manager, it's important to maintain a positive image of yourself and your team. This means being professional, courteous, and respectful at all times. It also means being proactive in seeking feedback and addressing concerns.

Maintaining a positive image of yourself and your team can help you build trust and respect with colleagues. It can also help you attract the best talent, retain employees, and create a positive work environment.

Conclusion

Understanding the organization is the foundation for effective management. By understanding the organizational structure, culture, goals, values, stakeholders, and relationships, managers can align their team's goals and priorities with those of the organization. They can also build relationships with colleagues across departments, build alliances with key players, and maintain a positive image of themselves and their team. In short, understanding the organization is essential for any manager who wants to succeed in today's complex business environment.

CHAPTER 3: COMMUNICATING EFFECTIVELY

Communication is an essential component of management. The ability to communicate effectively can make or break a project, team, or relationship. In this chapter, we will discuss the importance of communication in management, identify common communication barriers, explore different communication styles, and review active listening techniques. We'll also discuss methods for creating clear and concise messages, how to use non-verbal communication, and provide tips for giving and receiving feedback.

Importance of Communication in Management

Poor communication can create misunderstandings, confusion, and delays that can cost a company time and money. Effective communication is necessary for a team to be successful, regardless of their size, objectives, or location. Employees need to understand their roles, responsibilities, goals, and expectations. It is the manager's responsibility to ensure all team members communicate effectively and efficiently. By fostering an environment of open communication, team members can be empowered to share their ideas, concerns, and suggestions, which can improve morale, engagement, and productivity.

Barriers to Effective Communication

Effective communication is not always easy. There are many barriers that can prevent effective communication in the workplace. One such barrier is a lack of clarity in the message being communicated. If the message is vague or confusing, it can lead to misinterpretations. Other barriers to effective communication include language differences, cultural barriers, physical distance, and technical difficulties.

Different Communication Styles

There are many different communication styles. Each style represents different personality traits, habits, and preferences. Effective managers understand that different communication styles may require different approaches. Some individuals prefer direct, verbal communication, while others may prefer written communication. Additionally, some individuals may prefer to communicate in person, while others may prefer communication from a distance. By understanding these different communication styles, managers can adapt their communication style to better fit the needs of their team members.

Active Listening Techniques

Active listening is a critical component of effective communication. Active listening requires a person to listen attentively to what the other person is saying and provide feedback in a way that shows they have understood the message that is being conveyed. Active listening involves paying attention to body language, tone, and other non-verbal cues as well as what is being said.

Creating Clear and Concise Messages

Clear and concise messages are essential to effective

communication. Sending long, convoluted messages can lead to confusion and misunderstandings. Managers need to strike a balance between brevity and clarity when communicating with their teams. By doing so, they can ensure that their team members receive the message as intended.

Non-Verbal Communication

Non-verbal communication can be just as important as verbal communication. Non-verbal cues such as facial expressions, body language, and tone can convey meaning in ways that words cannot. Managers need to be aware of their non-verbal cues, as well as those of their team members, and how they may be perceived.

Written Communication Skills

Written communication is an important communication skill for managers. Effective written communication should be clear, concise, and well-organized. Managers should avoid using jargon and acronyms when communicating with their teams. They also need to be aware of their tone when writing emails and other documents.

Giving and Receiving Feedback

Effective feedback is essential for personal and professional growth and development. Feedback needs to be timely, specific and balanced. Managers should provide feedback to their team members regularly, both in positive and negative situations. Feedback should be constructive and designed to help the team member develop specific skills. Additionally, managers need to be open to receiving feedback from their team members and providing a safe environment for team members to offer their feedback.

In conclusion, effective communication is a fundamental tool for effective management. Managers need to understand and overcome common communication barriers, be aware of accommodating different communication styles, employ active listening techniques, and know-how to deliver clear and concise messages. Written communication skills and effective feedback techniques are essential to keeping employees informed and engaged. By utilizing these techniques, managers can build strong relationships with their team members, drive productivity, and ultimately lead their teams to success.

CHAPTER 4: BUILDING AND LEADING TEAMS

Effective team building and leadership can make or break an organization. A great manager should have a deep understanding of team dynamics and know how to foster and sustain a positive work environment. In this chapter, we will discuss the benefits of effective teams, the roles and responsibilities of team members, and the strategies for building, leading, and motivating high-performing teams.

Overview of team dynamics

Teams are groups of individuals brought together to accomplish a specific task or project. They can vary in size, scope, and complexity. Although the tasks or objectives may differ, every team has to deal with forming, norming, storming, and performing stages of development. It's important to note that teams evolve, and managers must be equipped to understand and manage each stage of development.

The first stage, forming, is the initial stage where team members get to know each other and establish roles and responsibilities. The norming stage is where planned tasks to reach the team's goals are clarified. The storming stage is where conflicts may arise amongst team members, but can be harnessed for good as a challenge to progress. The performing stage is where the team is working on high-performance mode. Teams that have been together for an extended period may experience a decline in enthusiasm and become comfortable with their work. Managers must be aware of this and continue to push innovation and brainstorming.

Benefits of effective teams

Effective teams play a key role in achieving organizational goals. A great manager must know how to build, lead, motivate, and sustain high-performing teams. Here are some of the benefits of effective teams:

❖ Innovation: Teams that collaborate and brainstorm are more likely to come up with unique and creative ideas.

❖ Increased productivity: When individuals work together to achieve a common goal, it is more likely that they can complete tasks more efficiently and effectively.

❖ Better decision-making: Teams can bring diverse perspectives to the table, resulting in better decisions.

❖ Increased job satisfaction: Working in a positive and effective team can lead to satisfaction and higher morale levels.

Roles and responsibilities of team members

A great manager who leads an effective team must understand the roles and responsibilities of each team member. Here are some of the key roles:

➢ Leader: This individual leads the team and makes strategic decisions.

➢ Creative force: This individual brings new and fresh ideas to the table.

➢ Quality control: This individual ensures that the work produced by the team is of the highest standard.

➢ Liaison: This individual is responsible for maintaining relationships both within and outside of the team.

➢ Task master: This individual is responsible for ensuring that tasks are executed and completed on time.

Building a diverse team

Great managers know that diversity is central to building successful teams. They understand that the best ideas may come from individuals with diverse perspectives and experiences. A diverse team can bring a range of thoughts and opinions to the table, which can result in more strategic decisions. Here are some tips for building a diverse team:

➢ Cast the net wide: Don't limit yourself to recruiting in the same places; explore diverse sources and networks.

➢ Create an inclusive environment: Encourage diversity and create an inclusive workspace.

➢ Focus on skills: Look for a range of skills and experiences that will benefit the team.

➢ Be aware of implicit biases: Watch for unconscious biases in the recruitment process.

➢ Promote diversity at all levels: Encourage diversity in your leadership team to promote inclusivity and avoid discrimination.

Strategies for motivating and engaging team members

Great managers should aim to motivate and engage their teams continuously to achieve their full potential. Here are some strategies that can help:

➢ Set clear goals and KPIs: Focus on achievable goals and communicate performance targets.

➤ Offer opportunities for development: Create opportunities for individuals to develop their skills.

➤ Recognize and reward achievements: celebrate individual and team accomplishments.

➤ Give feedback: Share feedback regularly for team members to improve and develop.

➤ Encourage teamwork: Foster a team culture and promote teamwork.

➤ Resolving conflicts within the team: Address conflicts as soon as they arise to maintain a positive team culture.

Leading by example

Leadership is an essential ingredient in building effective teams. A great leader should lead by example, setting the standards for the team to follow. Here are some fundamental traits of a great leader:

❖ Honesty and integrity: A great leader must demonstrate honesty and integrity.

❖ Communication skills: They should be effective communicators, both verbally and in writing.

❖ Adaptability: Adaptability in the face of change and uncertainty is key.

❖ Emotional intelligence: They need to be perceptive, empathetic, and have a good understanding of emotions.

❖ Responsibility: They should take responsibility for their actions and be willing to accept blame or criticism.

Creating a positive team culture

Successful teams thrive in a positive work environment. A team that has a positive culture is one where team members feel valued and are motivated to work towards the team's goals. Here are some tips on developing a positive team culture:

> ➢ Lead by example: Great managers must set a positive example.

> ➢ Encourage inclusivity: Create a welcoming workplace where diversity is embraced.

> ➢ Communicate effectively: Ensure open and honest communication throughout the team.

> ➢ Recognize and celebrate successes: Celebrate successes as a team; this should create a sense of pride and ownership in each team member.

> ➢ Listen to suggestions: Encourage and listen to suggestions from team members; this will create an environment that welcomes innovation and creativity.

> ➢ Have fun: Encourage fun activities and team building exercises that will help to foster a positive and united team culture.

Conclusion:

Building and leading successful teams is a crucial component of great management. Teams that work well together can drive the organization towards its goals. As such, managers should invest in developing their skills and understanding of team dynamics. This will allow them to build, lead, and motivate diverse teams positively. The strategies outlined in this chapter offer a starting point for managers to create successful teams that drive positive outcomes for the organization.

CHAPTER 5: MANAGING CHANGE

Change is an inevitable part of any organization's growth and development. Whether it's a shift in technology, strategy, or structure, change is necessary to stay competitive and relevant in the market. However, managing change can be a daunting task for managers and employees alike. In this chapter, we will explore how to manage change effectively to minimize disruption and ensure the success of the organization.

Definition of change management

Change management refers to the process of preparing, supporting, and managing changes to the organization. It involves identifying the need for change, planning how to implement it, executing the change, and finally, evaluating its effectiveness. The goal of change management is to minimize the negative impacts of change and maximize its benefits.

Reasons for change

There are many reasons why an organization may need to undergo a change. It could be due to internal factors such as a shift in strategy, a change in leadership, or a desire to improve efficiency. Alternatively, external factors such as economic changes, advances in technology, or shifts in customer preferences could drive change. Regardless of the reason, it's important to understand the drivers of change to ensure that the change is necessary and aligned with the organization's goals.

Preparing for changes

Successful change management requires careful planning and preparation. The first step is to identify the need for change and the desired outcomes. Next, it's important to involve key stakeholders, such as employees, customers, and suppliers, in the process to gain buy-in and support. It's also crucial to assess the organization's readiness for change, including its culture, resources, and capacity to handle the change.

Implementing changes effectively

Implementing change requires clear communication, a well-defined plan, and effective leadership. The plan should include specific steps, timelines, and roles and responsibilities. Communication should be ongoing and transparent to keep all stakeholders informed and engaged. Leaders should also model the desired behaviors and address any resistance or concerns from employees.

Supporting employees during times of change

Change can be stressful and uncertain for employees. As a manager, it's important to provide support and resources to help them navigate the change. This could include training, coaching, and counseling. Recognizing and celebrating employees' efforts and successes during the change process can also help to build morale and motivation.

Overcoming resistance to change

Resistance to change is common and can arise for a variety of reasons, including fear of the unknown, lack of trust in leadership, or concerns about job security. To overcome resistance, it's important to involve employees in the change process and communicate the benefits of the change. Leaders should also address any concerns or questions employees may have and provide a safe environment for employees to express their opinions and feelings.

Measuring the success of change

To determine the success of the change, it's essential to set clear goals and objectives and measure progress against them. This could involve tracking metrics such as employee satisfaction, productivity, or revenue. It's also important to solicit feedback from stakeholders and evaluate the effectiveness of the change on an ongoing basis.

Evolving with technological changes

One of the most common drivers of change is advances in technology. To stay competitive, organizations must be willing to adapt and evolve with these changes. This could involve investing in new technology, updating existing systems, or developing new skills and capabilities. It's important for managers to stay up-to-date on emerging technologies and trends and to anticipate how they may impact the organization in the future.

In conclusion, managing change is a critical skill for managers. With the right planning, communication, and leadership, change can be a positive force for growth and development. By involving employees, providing support, and measuring progress, managers can ensure that the organization is well-positioned for success in the future.

CHAPTER 6:
SETTING GOALS
AND OBJECTIVES

As a manager, setting goals and objectives is critical to ensure success for yourself, your team, and the organization as a whole. Goals provide direction, focus, and motivation for what you and your team are trying to achieve. Objectives are specific, measurable, and time-bound goals that help you track progress and identify areas for improvement.

Importance of setting goals and objectives:

Setting goals and objectives is important for several reasons. Goals provide a sense of direction for the team and help them understand what they are working towards. They motivate team members to work towards a common objective and give employees a sense of accomplishment when they achieve something. Goals provide focus to the team and help them prioritize their work.

Identifying key performance indicators:

Key Performance Indicators (KPIs) are specific measures that are used to evaluate the performance of an organization or an individual. You need to identify the KPIs that matter to your team and align those KPIs with organizational goals. Examples of

KPIs could be increased sales revenue, reduced employee turnover, increased customer satisfaction rate, and so on. You should also identify leading KPIs that help predict future performance.

Setting SMART goals:

SMART goals are specific, measurable, achievable, relevant, and time-bound goals. It is essential to set SMART goals for your team to ensure that they stay on track. Specific goals are clearly defined and leave no room for ambiguity. Measurable goals should be tied to KPIs to track progress. Achievable goals are realistic and attainable for the team. Relevant goals are aligned with the company's objectives. Time-bound goals have a specific deadline attached to them.

Aligning individual and team goals with organizational goals:

It is essential to ensure that team goals and individual goals align with organizational goals. This alignment helps create a sense of purpose and direction for the team. It also helps employees understand their contribution to the bigger picture.

Creating action plans:

Creating action plans is an integral part of achieving goals. You need to break down large goals into smaller, achievable steps and create a plan for how to accomplish each step. This process makes the goal more manageable and increases the chances of successful implementation.

Tracking progress and making adjustments:

Tracking progress is critical to ensure that you stay on track to achieve your goals. Regular check-ins with the team help identify problem areas and make necessary adjustments. It is essential to stay agile to adjust goals and objectives when conditions change.

Celebrating successes:

Celebrating successes is crucial to maintain team motivation and morale. Celebrating small wins along the way can provide a sense of accomplishment and encourage continued effort.

Learning from failures:

Sometimes, goals are not achieved. It is essential to learn from failures and use them as the basis for future success. Encourage your team to view failures as a stepping stone to success and to learn from their mistakes.

Setting goals and objectives is an essential aspect of managing a team. Prioritizing goal-setting, identifying key performance indicators, setting SMART goals, aligning individual and team goals with organizational goals, creating action plans, tracking progress, celebrating successes, and learning from failures, can all help you become an effective manager.

CHAPTER 7:
MANAGING TIME
AND PRIORITIES

Time is the most precious resource we have, and as managers, we have a lot on our plates. From setting goals to managing teams and handling crises, it can be challenging to manage time effectively. In this chapter, we will discuss some strategies to help you manage your time and priorities better.

Overview of time management

Time management is the process of organizing and planning how much time to spend on specific activities. Effective time management allows you to complete tasks efficiently and reduce stress. The first step in effective time management is to identify your priorities.

Identifying priorities

Identifying your priorities is crucial in managing your time effectively. As a manager, your time is valuable, and you must focus on tasks with the highest priority. For instance, managing your team's performance takes precedence over answering emails or attending meetings that do not align with your objectives.

To identify priorities, you should start by setting goals. What do you want to achieve? This could be personal or organizational goals. Once you have identified your goal, break it down into smaller objectives and rank them in order of importance. This will help you prioritize your tasks effectively.

Creating a schedule

Creating a schedule is essential in managing your time effectively. A schedule gives structure to your day and ensures you allocate enough time to important tasks. When creating your schedule, you should dedicate time to high-priority tasks first. For instance, if you have a critical report to complete, schedule time in your day to work on it.

Another important factor to consider when creating your schedule is your energy levels. It's best to schedule difficult tasks when you are most alert and energetic. For many people, this is often early in the morning.

Using technology for time management

Technology has made time management more accessible than ever. Many tools and apps can help you manage your time more effectively. For instance, there are apps that can help you plan your day or schedule reminders, such as setting alarms or push notifications for important tasks and deadlines.

Project management tools like Asana or Trello are also valuable tools to keep track of your projects and collaborate with team members.

Delegating tasks to others

As a manager, it's natural to feel the need to control everything. However, delegation is essential in effective time management. Delegating tasks to others ensures that you can focus on important tasks that require your attention.

When delegating, it's important to ensure that the delegated tasks align with the employee's skills and capabilities. Clear communication is also critical to ensure that the employee understands what is expected of them. Additionally, it's essential to provide support, guidance, and feedback to ensure that the delegated tasks are completed successfully.

Avoiding procrastination

Procrastination is the enemy of good time management. It's easy to get caught up in minor tasks or get sidetracked by social media or other distractions. To avoid procrastination, it's important to eliminate distractions and create an environment that is conducive to work.

One way to do this is to use the Pomodoro technique, where you divide your workday into short intervals of work and breaks. This technique helps you stay focused on work and ensures that you take regular breaks to recharge.

Managing interruptions

Interruptions can disrupt your workflow and reduce productivity. However, it's almost impossible to eliminate all interruptions, especially in a busy work environment. Therefore, it's important to manage interruptions effectively. One way to do this is to communicate boundaries to your team members or colleagues. For instance, you can inform them when you're available for meetings or request that they send an email instead of approaching you.

Another approach is to prioritize interruptions. For instance, if a team member requires feedback or has an urgent issue, it's essential to prioritize their interruption over a less urgent matter.

Balancing work and personal life

Finally, it's essential to achieve a balance between work and personal life for effective time management. Overworking can lead to burnout and reduced productivity. Therefore, it's important to set boundaries and ensure that you allocate enough time for personal activities, such as hobbies or spending time with family and friends.

In conclusion, managing time and priorities is essential for effective management. You should identify your priorities, create a schedule that is efficient and effective, use technology to assist with time management, delegate tasks to others, avoid procrastination, manage interruptions, and maintain a healthy work-life balance. By managing time and priorities effectively, you can enhance productivity, reduce stress levels, and achieve your goals.

CHAPTER 8: PROBLEM-SOLVING AND DECISION-MAKING

One of the most important skills that a manager must develop is problem-solving and decision-making. These skills are necessary for a manager to navigate difficult situations in the workplace and implement changes that can benefit the organization and its employees.

In this chapter, we will explore the steps involved in effective problem-solving and decision-making, from identifying problems to evaluating the effectiveness of solutions. We'll also look at how to learn from mistakes along the way.

Step 1: Identifying problems

The first step to effective problem-solving is to identify the problem. This may seem obvious, but often managers can get caught up in symptoms of a problem without realizing the root cause. It is important to identify the problem accurately in order to develop an effective solution.

When identifying the problem, it is important to ask questions, gather information, and understand the history of the issue. This can help to identify the underlying causes of the problem. It is also important to consider the impact of the problem on employees, customers, and the organization as a whole.

Step 2: Analyzing the situation

Once the problem has been identified, it is time to analyze the situation. This involves further investigation to understand the extent of the problem and its causes. The goal is to develop a clear understanding of the problem so that a solution can be developed that addresses the root cause.

When analyzing the situation, it is important to look at both qualitative and quantitative data. Data can help to identify trends and patterns that can be used to inform solutions. It is also important to involve others in the analysis process, seeking input and perspectives from colleagues and team members.

Step 3: Developing alternatives

With a clear understanding of the problem, it is time to develop alternative solutions. This involves brainstorming ideas and considering different approaches to address the problem. It is important to consider both short-term and long-term solutions, as well as the feasibility of each option.

When developing alternatives, it can be helpful to involve others in the process. This can help to generate more ideas and also increase buy-in for any solutions that are implemented.

Step 4: Evaluating options

Once alternative solutions have been developed, it is time to evaluate the options. This involves considering the pros and cons of each solution, as well as the potential risks and benefits. It is important to consider the impact of each solution on employees, customers, and the organization overall.

When evaluating options, it can be helpful to use a decision-making framework or criteria to guide the evaluation process. This can help to ensure that all important factors are considered when making a decision.

Step 5: Making decisions

With alternative solutions evaluated, it is time to make a decision on which solution to implement. This involves choosing the solution that is the best fit for the problem and aligns with the overall goals and objectives of the organization.

When making decisions, it is important to communicate with stakeholders and ensure that they are aware of the decision and why it was made. It can also be helpful to create a plan for implementing the solution and ensuring that employees and teams are aware of the plan and their roles.

Step 6: Implementing solutions

Once a decision has been made, it is time to implement the solution. This involves taking action and putting the plan into action. It is important to communicate with employees and team members and ensure that they are aware of the plan and their roles.

When implementing a solution, it is important to monitor progress and make adjustments as needed. It is also important to ensure that resources are allocated appropriately and that all necessary steps are taken to ensure the success of the solution.

Step 7: Evaluating the effectiveness of solutions

After a solution has been implemented, it is important to evaluate its effectiveness. This involves considering whether the solution effectively addressed the problem, as well as its impact on employees, customers, and the organization overall.

When evaluating the effectiveness of solutions, it is important to use data and metrics to track progress and measure success. This can help to identify areas for improvement and make adjustments as needed.

Step 8: Learning from mistakes

Even the most effective managers will make mistakes from time to time. The key is to learn from those mistakes and use them as an opportunity for growth and development.

When mistakes are made, it is important to take responsibility for them and work to make changes that will prevent them from happening again in the future. This may involve seeking feedback from others and being open to constructive criticism.

Conclusion

Problem-solving and decision-making are critical skills for any manager to develop. By following the steps outlined in this chapter, managers can effectively identify and address problems, make tough decisions, and learn from mistakes along the way. By leveraging these skills, managers can help to drive growth and success for their organization, while also building a positive and effective workplace culture.

CHAPTER 9: MANAGING PERFORMANCE

Effective performance management is key to building a successful team. As a manager, it is important to communicate clear expectations, provide feedback, and recognize and address areas in need of improvement. In this chapter, we will explore strategies for managing performance that will help you drive your team's success.

Defining Performance Management

Performance management is the process of setting goals, monitoring progress, and providing feedback to help employees achieve success. It involves identifying areas of strength and areas in need of improvement, coaching employees, and recognizing good performance.

As a manager, it is important to make sure employees know what is expected of them. Establishing clear goals and metrics for success will help employees understand what they need to do to achieve success. Additionally, it is important to provide ongoing feedback and coaching to help employees stay on track and improve their performance.

Setting Expectations

To establish clear expectations, managers should set specific, measurable, achievable, relevant, and time-bound (SMART) goals for their employees. Each goal should have specific metrics for success and should be aligned with the company's overall objectives.

Make sure to communicate these expectations to your team early on, and revisit them regularly to ensure everyone is on the same page. By setting clear expectations, you provide employees with a roadmap for success.

Providing Feedback

Providing ongoing feedback is essential to managing performance. It is important to offer both positive feedback and constructive criticism. When providing feedback, be specific, objective, and focus on behavior rather than personality.

Employees want to know what they are doing well and areas in need of improvement, so they can continue to grow and develop in their roles. Make sure to provide feedback in a timely manner, and offer support to help employees improve.

Conducting Performance Reviews

Performance reviews are an important part of the performance management process. They allow managers to evaluate an employee's progress over the past year, assess their strengths and weaknesses, and set goals for the coming year.

During performance reviews, it is important to provide specific examples of an employee's achievement or areas in need of improvement. Make sure to engage employees in the process by asking them to self-assess and providing them with the opportunity to give feedback.

Coaching Employees

Coaching is a continuous process of providing feedback and support to help employees develop their skills and improve their performance. It involves providing employees with resources and guidance to help them succeed.

As a coach, it is important to be supportive and approachable. Make sure to set aside time for one-on-one meetings to discuss progress and offer guidance. Encourage employees to seek your support and provide them with the resources they need to be successful.

Recognizing and Rewarding Good Performance

Recognizing and rewarding good performance is a powerful motivator. It helps employees feel valued and appreciated, and reinforces the behaviors that drive success.

When recognizing good performance, be specific and timely. Share examples of what the employee did well and how it contributed to the team or company. Also, consider offering rewards such as bonuses, promotions, or meaningful opportunities for growth and development.

Addressing Poor Performance

Addressing poor performance can be challenging, but it is an essential part of managing performance. It is important to approach the situation with empathy and objectivity, and address the behavior rather than the person.

When addressing poor performance, provide specific examples of what the employee needs to improve and offer guidance on how to do so. Be supportive and offer resources to help the employee improve.

Maintaining Confidentiality

When managing performance, it is important to maintain confidentiality. Employees want to be assured that their privacy will be respected, so it is important to keep all performance-related discussions confidential.

Make sure to only share performance-related information on a need-to-know basis, and be clear with employees about what information will be shared and with whom. Maintaining confidentiality will help build trust with your team, and foster a culture of open communication.

Managing performance requires managers to provide clear expectations, ongoing feedback, and support to help employees achieve success. By establishing a culture of employee development and support, managers can create a team that is motivated, engaged, and ready to take on any challenge.

CHAPTER 10: MOTIVATING EMPLOYEES

As a manager, it is important to understand that motivation plays a key role in achieving business goals and objectives. Motivated employees are more productive, engaged, and satisfied with their work. However, motivating employees is not a one-size-fits-all approach. Each employee has different values, interests, and motivations, and as a manager, it is your responsibility to uncover what motivates them and create a work environment that fosters motivation. In this chapter, we will explore the different theories of motivation, how to identify what motivates employees, and how to create a motivating work environment.

Overview of Motivation

Motivation is the driving force that inspires individuals to take action and achieve their goals. In the workplace, motivation can be intrinsic or extrinsic. Intrinsic motivation comes from within an individual due to the pleasure, satisfaction, or sense of accomplishment they get from completing a task. Extrinsic motivation, on the other hand, comes from external factors such as rewards or recognition. While extrinsic motivation can be effective in some situations, it is important to foster intrinsic motivation in the workplace since it leads to increased creativity, improved problem-solving abilities, and higher job satisfaction.

Motivation Theories

There are numerous motivation theories in the field of management. Some of the most prominent theories include Maslow's Hierarchy of Needs, Alderfer's ERG Theory, Herzberg's Two-Factor Theory, and McClelland's Three Needs Theory. Understanding these theories will help managers uncover what motivates their employees and create a work environment that fosters motivation.

Maslow's Hierarchy of Needs states that individuals have five basic needs: physiological, safety, love and belonging, esteem, and self-actualization. According to Maslow, individuals will only seek to satisfy higher needs when the lower needs have been met. For example, employees who are struggling to meet their physiological or safety needs will not be motivated to work towards self-actualization until those basic needs are met.

Alderfer's ERG Theory is a modification of Maslow's theory. Alderfer divided the five needs into three categories: Existence, Relatedness, and Growth. Existence needs include the basic needs of Maslow's physiological and safety needs. Relatedness needs are similar to Maslow's love and belonging needs, and Growth needs are the same as Maslow's esteem and self-actualization needs. Alderfer's theory allows managers to recognize that sometimes employees' basic needs need to be met before they are motivated to work towards higher level needs.

Herzberg's Two-Factor Theory asserts that there are two types of factors in the workplace that affect motivation and job satisfaction: hygiene factors and motivators. Hygiene factors include working conditions, job security, and salary. While hygiene factors don't necessarily improve motivation, their absence can cause dissatisfaction in employees. On the other hand, motivators include factors such as recognition, opportunities for growth, and meaningful work. These factors lead to increased job satisfaction and motivation.

McClelland's Three Needs Theory states that individuals are motivated by three needs: achievement, affiliation, and power. According to this theory, individuals with a high need for achievement are driven by taking on challenging tasks and setting goals for themselves. Employees with a high need for affiliation seek to establish strong relationships with their colleagues and are more motivated by collaborative work. Individuals with a high need for power desire to be in control and to have an influence over others.

Identifying What Motivates Employees

As a manager, it is important to understand that each employee has different motivations and therefore, it is essential to identify what motivates each individual. Here are some strategies to help uncover what motivates employees:

- ❖ Conduct one-on-one meetings: Regular check-ins with employees can help them feel valued and understood. During these meetings, ask open-ended questions to understand what motivates them.

- ❖ Observe employee behavior: Observe how employees complete their tasks and what parts of their job they seem to enjoy the most.

- ❖ Review previous performance metrics: Reviewing past performance metrics can help identify which employees excel in which areas.

- ❖ Ask employees directly: Sometimes asking employees directly what motivates them is the most straightforward approach.

Creating a Motivating Work Environment

Creating a motivating work environment is key to retaining employees and achieving business goals. Here are some strategies for creating a motivating work environment:

❖   Encouraging teamwork: Encouraging teamwork and collaboration can help individuals feel valued and connected to their colleagues.

❖   Offering opportunities for growth and development: Offering opportunities for growth and development helps employees feel like their contributions are valued and that there is room for advancement within the organization.

❖   Providing incentives and rewards: Providing incentives and rewards for excellent performance can help motivate employees.

❖   Building a sense of purpose: Building a sense of purpose within the organization can lead to increased motivation and job satisfaction.

❖   Balancing recognition and challenges: While recognition for a job well done is important, too much recognition can lead to complacency. Challenging employees with new tasks and responsibilities can help foster growth and maintain motivation.

Conclusion

Motivating employees is a critical part of being a great manager. Understanding the different theories of motivation and what motivates individual employees can help create a work environment that fosters motivation. A motivating work environment encourages teamwork, offers opportunities for growth and development, provides incentives and rewards, builds a sense of purpose, and balances recognition with challenges. By following the strategies outlined in this chapter, managers can motivate their employees, improve productivity, and achieve business goals and objectives.

CHAPTER 11:
NEGOTIATION SKILLS

As a manager, negotiating is an essential skill to possess. It is impossible to avoid negotiations in business, whether it is with employees, clients, vendors, or other stakeholders. To be a great manager, it is vital to know how to negotiate effectively and achieve the desired result without damaging relationships.

Definition of negotiation

Negotiation is a process by which two or more parties make compromises and come to an agreement. It involves exchanging ideas, information, and proposals to reach a mutually beneficial outcome. In negotiation, it is crucial to understand that both parties have something to gain and something to lose. A successful negotiation is one in which both parties feel satisfied with the outcome.

Types of negotiation

There are two types of negotiation: distributive and integrative.

Distributive negotiation, also known as competitive or positional negotiation, is a win-lose negotiation. In this type of negotiation, the parties involved try to get the most out of the negotiation and are often confrontational. It is common in situations where parties have conflicting interests, such as buying a car or negotiating a salary.

Integrative negotiation, also known as collaborative or interest-based negotiation, is a win-win negotiation. In this type of negotiation, the parties involved work together to create value and maximize gains. It is common in situations where parties have shared interests, such as resolving a dispute or negotiating a contract.

Preparing for negotiation

Preparation is key to a successful negotiation. Before the negotiation, it is crucial to identify your objectives, priorities, and limits. Researching the other party's objectives, priorities, and limits can help you understand their perspective and use it to find common ground.

Building rapport

Building rapport is crucial in negotiation, as it helps you establish trust and a positive relationship with the other party. In the beginning, take some time to engage in small talk, listen carefully, and find common ground. Avoid being aggressive or confrontational, as it can create a hostile environment and damage the negotiations.

Identifying positions and interests

In negotiation, it is essential to distinguish between positions and interests. Positions are the stated demands of each party, while interests are the underlying motivations. Understanding the other party's interests can help you find creative solutions that meet both parties' needs.

Finding common ground

Finding common ground is crucial in integrative negotiation. Based on the interests identified, look for ways to create value and maximize gains. This requires creativity, openness, and a willingness to compromise.

Developing alternatives

Developing alternatives is crucial in case the negotiation fails. It is essential to consider your BATNA (Best Alternative to a Negotiated Agreement), a term coined by Harvard Business School professor Roger Fisher. Having a reasonable BATNA provides you with leverage in the negotiation and enables you to walk away from a bad deal.

Closing the deal

Closing the deal involves reaching a mutually beneficial agreement. It is essential to summarize the agreement and put it in writing to avoid misunderstandings. Follow-up communication after the negotiation is essential to ensure that both parties are satisfied with the agreement.

Conclusion:

Negotiation is a critical skill in management, and being a great manager requires mastering negotiation techniques. Effective negotiation involves identifying common interests, finding creative solutions, and closing the deal. With preparation, creativity, and an open mindset, managers can achieve their desired outcome without damaging relationships. Remember, negotiation is an opportunity to create value, build relationships, and make a positive impact on the organization.

CHAPTER 12:
ETHICAL AND LEGAL
CONSIDERATIONS

When it comes to management, ethics and legality are two of the most important considerations to keep in mind. A good manager must be able to maintain a high degree of ethical and legal responsibility for the well-being of their team and the company as a whole. In this chapter, we will discuss the importance of ethical and legal considerations in management and explore common ethical dilemmas that managers face.

Importance of Ethical and Legal Considerations

As a manager, it is important to ensure that all employees are treated fairly, regardless of their background or position. Ethical considerations help to create a positive work environment where trust and respect are valued. In addition, adherence to ethical standards ensures that the company operates in a way that is consistent with its values and principles.

Legal considerations are equally important. Laws and regulations exist to protect employees and ensure that companies operate in a fair and equitable manner. As a manager, it is your responsibility to ensure that your team adheres to all applicable laws and regulations.

Common Ethical Dilemmas in Management

As a manager, you are likely to encounter a variety of ethical dilemmas. Some common ethical dilemmas that managers face are:

- ❖ Conflict of Interest: As a manager, you may be faced with situations where your personal interests conflict with the interests of the company or your team. It is important to identify potential conflicts of interest and take steps to avoid them.

- ❖ Confidentiality: Managers must be aware of their responsibility to protect confidential information. Breaching confidentiality can damage the reputation of the company and erode trust among team members.

- ❖ Discrimination: Managers must ensure that all employees are treated equally, regardless of their race, gender, age, or other factors. Discrimination can lead to lowered morale and legal consequences.

- ❖ Harassment: Employees have the right to work in an environment that is free from harassment. As a manager, it is your responsibility to prevent harassment and create a safe and respectful work environment.

- ❖ Ethical Dilemmas with Clients: At times, managers may be faced with ethical dilemmas involving clients. It is important to consider the best interests of the company and its values when making decisions.

Understanding Laws and Regulations

As a manager, it is important to ensure that your team is aware of all relevant laws and regulations. This includes labor laws, health and safety regulations, and data protection laws. Ignorance of the law is not an excuse for non-compliance.

Avoiding Discrimination

One of the most important ethical considerations for managers is to avoid discrimination. Discrimination can take many forms, including race, gender, age, disability, religion, and sexual orientation. Managers must ensure that all employees are treated fairly and equally.

Managers should take steps to avoid discrimination, including:

> ➤ Providing equal opportunities for all employees, regardless of their background or position.

> ➤ Ensuring that performance evaluations are based on objective criteria rather than subjective judgments.

> ➤ Ensuring that the selection process for hiring, promotions, and other opportunities is free from bias.

> ➤ Creating an environment that is welcoming to all employees, regardless of their background.

Building a Culture of Integrity

Integrity is an important aspect of ethical behavior. A culture of integrity is one where all employees hold themselves and others to high ethical standards. Managers play a crucial role in building and maintaining a culture of integrity.

To build a culture of integrity, managers should:

> ➤ Lead by example: Managers should model ethical behavior and encourage others to do the same.

> ➤ Educate employees: It is important to educate employees about the company's values, policies, and ethical standards.

> ➤ Encourage open communication: Creating an environment

where employees feel comfortable sharing their ethical concerns can help to prevent ethical lapses.

➤ Enforce ethical standards: Managers should enforce the company's ethical standards and take disciplinary action when necessary.

Conclusion

In this chapter, we explored the importance of ethical and legal considerations in management. We discussed some common ethical dilemmas that managers face and the importance of adhering to laws and regulations. We also explored how managers can avoid discrimination and build a culture of integrity. As a manager, it is your responsibility to set the tone for ethical behavior and ensure that your team operates in a fair and equitable manner.

CHAPTER 13: MANAGING DIVERSITY

Being a great manager means working with a diverse group of employees. Diversity refers to differences in terms of race, ethnicity, gender, age, sexual orientation, religion, disability, and other aspects of an employee's identity. Managing diversity is about promoting inclusivity, respecting differences, and avoiding discrimination.

Definition of diversity:

Diversity is crucial to any successful organization because it brings different perspectives, ideas, and experiences to the table. Thus, it is important to manage diversity effectively in the workplace. When individuals from diverse backgrounds work together, they bring new ways of thinking and better ways to address complex issues.

Benefits of diversity in the workplace:

Diversity benefits organizations in various ways. For instance, it helps to boost creativity and innovation, improves decision-making processes, enhances critical thinking, and strengthens problem-solving abilities. Moreover, it leads to better performance, higher employee engagement, motivation, and satisfaction.

Understanding different cultures:

Evaluating cultural differences is essential to manage diversity. One way of understanding cultural differences is by researching the country's history, values, norms, and beliefs. Additionally, it is important to recognize that culture is not limited to nationalities, but it refers to shared values, beliefs, and attributes that groups of people have.

Addressing stereotypes:

To manage diversity explicitly, it is essential to address stereotypes, prejudice, and discrimination. Stereotyping is when one assumes that someone possesses certain traits because of their membership of a particular group. Stereotyping and discrimination are harmful, as they create a hostile work environment for employees.

Promoting inclusivity:

Promoting inclusivity is one of the key aspects of managing diversity. Inclusivity means making everyone feel accepted, appreciated, and valued, irrespective of their background or identity. One way to accomplish this is by organizing events or forums that bring employees together to celebrate cultural diversity.

Encouraging open communication:

Communication is the foundation for promoting diversity in the workplace. Thus, ensuring open communication channels between employees of diverse backgrounds helps to understand one another better. Encouraging open communication allows employees to express themselves more freely without fear of judgment or prejudice.

Respecting individual differences:

Respect individual differences means valuing individual differences, such as personality traits, work styles, and communication styles. It is important to train employees on how to appreciate individual differences rather than using them to create conflicts or bias.

Avoiding discrimination:

Managing diversity requires avoiding discrimination or biases based on a person's identity, ethnicity, or gender. Discrimination or biases can create a hostile and toxic work environment. Thus, managers need to foster inclusivity by promoting diversity and ensuring adherence to the company's policy on diversity.

In conclusion, managing diversity involves creating an inclusive and welcoming work environment that ensures that every employee feels valued, appreciated, and respected. Promoting diversity means understanding cultural differences, addressing stereotypes, promoting inclusivity, and avoiding discrimination. By managing diversity, managers can enhance creativity, innovation, decision-making, and create a more diverse and better performing team.

CHAPTER 14: MANAGING PERFORMANCE AND STRESS

Managers are responsible for maintaining a productive and efficient work environment, which requires managing both employee performance and stress levels. Employees who experience high levels of stress are likely to experience a decrease in productivity and job satisfaction, leading to decreased job performance. In this chapter, we will explore strategies for identifying and managing performance issues caused by stress, as well as promoting employee well-being to prevent stress-related performance issues.

Understanding the Effects of Stress on Performance

Stress is a natural response to challenging situations, but excessive stress can lead to physical, mental, and emotional health issues, affecting productivity and employee engagement. Stress-related issues can be caused by various factors, including workload, job demands, lack of job security, poor working conditions, inadequate compensation, and ineffective leadership. As a manager, it's crucial to recognize the symptoms of stress-related performance issues in your employees.

Identifying Signs of Stress in Employees

The first step in managing stress is identifying its symptoms in employees. Common signs of stress can include physical symptoms like headaches, fatigue, and muscle tension, emotional symptoms like irritability, anxiety, and depression, and behavioral symptoms like increased absenteeism, decreased work performance, and mood changes. Managers should look for these signs and address them proactively to prevent negative consequences.

Helping Employees Manage Stress

Managers can help employees manage stress by offering resources and support for stress management. Such support can include offering flexible schedules, improving work-life balance, and providing training on stress management techniques, like time management and relaxation techniques. Managers should also encourage employees to maintain a healthy lifestyle by promoting physical activity, healthy eating, and adequate rest. Managers can demonstrate their support by listening to employees and offering solutions to resolve any sources of stress.

Creating a Supportive Work Environment

Creating a supportive work environment is one of the most effective ways of managing stress-related performance issues. This requires creating opportunities for employees to provide feedback, fostering relationships that encourage open communication, and building a culture that supports employee well-being. A supportive work environment provides employees with the space to express their thoughts and feelings, which helps them manage stress and feel more engaged in their work.

Providing Resources for Stress Management

As a manager, you have the responsibility to provide resources for stress management to ensure that employees receive the support they need. This can include counseling services, wellness programs, and access to mental health resources. Managers can also offer training on stress management techniques, performing stress management exercises as a group, or encouraging employees to participate in mindfulness activities like meditation. By investing in the health of employees, you are also investing in the success of the organization.

Encouraging Work-Life Balance

Achieving a work-life balance is crucial in managing stress-related performance issues. Employees who have a healthy balance between their work and personal life are more productive, motivated, and engaged in their work. Managers should encourage work-life balance by offering flexible schedules, remote work options, and support for childcare services. Encouraging employees to take breaks, eat lunch, and take time off is also vital in promoting work-life balance.

Promoting Physical Health

Physical health is an essential component of employee well-being. Managers should promote physical health by eliminating situations that can lead to physical harm or encouraging physical activity. This can include arranging ergonomic workspaces, offering standing desks, encouraging movement during the workday, or promoting participation in health-related programs like exercise or weight-loss programs. Managers should also provide access to healthcare resources like annual physical, mental health services, and preventive screenings.

Ensuring Employee Well-being

Employee well-being is critical in managing stress-related

performance issues. Managers can ensure employee well-being by facilitating work-life balance, reducing job demands that can lead to stress, supporting the adoption of healthy habits, offering resources for stress management, and building a culture that supports well-being. Managers should prioritize the well-being of employees in decision-making and lead by example.

Conclusion

Managing stress-related performance issues is essential in maintaining a productive and motivated workforce. Effective management of stress requires identifying signs in employees, helping them manage stress, creating a supportive work environment, providing resources for stress management, encouraging work-life balance, promoting physical health, and ensuring employee well-being. By investing in the well-being of employees, you are investing in the success of the organization.

CHAPTER 15: FINANCIAL MANAGEMENT

As a manager, it's important to understand the financial aspect of your organization. While numbers and spreadsheets may not be your thing, a basic understanding of financial management can help you make better decisions and improve your overall effectiveness. In this chapter, we'll cover the basics of financial management and how you can use this knowledge to make informed decisions.

Importance of Financial Management

Financial management is the process of managing an organization's financial resources, including budgeting, forecasting, and investing. It's important for managers to have a basic understanding of financial management, as it can help them make better decisions that benefit the organization and its stakeholders.

By understanding the financial health of the organization, managers can identify areas where they can reduce expenses and improve profitability. This knowledge can help managers make informed decisions about investments, staffing, and other critical areas of the organization. Additionally, understanding financial statements and performance metrics can help managers identify trends and make adjustments to improve the bottom line.

Understanding Financial Statements

Financial statements provide a snapshot of an organization's financial health. They include the income statement, balance sheet, and cash flow statement. Each of these statements provides important information that managers can use to make informed decisions.

The income statement shows the revenue earned and expenses incurred over a specific period. It's used to determine the profitability of the organization and is often used to make decisions about investments, staffing, and other areas of the organization.

The balance sheet shows the assets and liabilities of the organization at a specific point in time. It's used to determine the financial health of the organization and is often used to make decisions about borrowing, investing, and other critical financial decisions.

The cash flow statement shows the inflow and outflow of cash over a specific period. It's used to determine the organization's liquidity and is often used to make decisions about borrowing, investing, and other financial decisions.

Analyzing Performance Metrics

Performance metrics provide a way for managers to track the financial health of their organizations. Metrics such as return on investment (ROI), profit margin, and cash flow can help managers identify areas where they can reduce expenses and improve revenue.

ROI measures the return on investment for a specific project or investment. It's used to determine the profitability of the investment and is often used to make decisions about future investments.

Profit margin measures the profitability of the organization. It's calculated by dividing net profit by revenue and is used to identify areas where the organization can reduce expenses and improve profitability.

Cash flow measures the inflow and outflow of cash over a specific period. It's used to determine the organization's liquidity and is often used to make decisions about borrowing, investing, and other critical financial decisions.

Budgeting and Forecasting

Budgeting and forecasting are critical components of financial management. A budget is a plan for how a company plans to allocate resources over a specific period. It's often used to make decisions about staffing, investments, and other critical areas of the organization.

Forecasting is the process of predicting future events. It's often used to predict revenue, expenses, and other key financial metrics. By forecasting future events, managers can make informed decisions about investments, staffing, and other critical areas of the organization.

Managing Cash flow

Managing cash flow is critical to the financial health of an organization. Cash flow is the inflow and outflow of cash over a specific period. It's important to maintain a positive cash flow to ensure the organization has the cash it needs to pay its bills and make investments.

To manage cash flow, managers should focus on reducing expenses, increasing revenue, and managing inventory. Additionally, managers should ensure that customers pay their bills on time, and they should consider financing options to cover short-term cash flow gaps.

Investing in the Organization

Investing in the organization is critical to its long-term success. Managers should consider investing in new technology, equipment, and research and development. These investments can help the organization reduce expenses and improve revenue over time.

When considering investments, managers should weigh the potential benefits against the costs. They should also consider the organization's overall financial health, including its liquidity, profitability, and cash flow.

Reducing Expenses

Reducing expenses is one of the best ways to improve the financial health of an organization. Managers should focus on reducing unnecessary expenses while maintaining the quality of products and services.

To reduce expenses, managers should look for ways to streamline processes, improve efficiency, and eliminate waste. They should also consider outsourcing certain functions to reduce staffing and overhead costs.

Measuring Return on Investment

Measuring return on investment is critical to making informed financial decisions. ROI measures the return on investment for a specific project or investment. It's used to determine the profitability of the investment and is often used to make decisions about future investments.

To measure ROI, managers should compare the cost of the investment to the revenue it generates. They should also consider the long-term benefits of the investment, such as increased efficiency or improved customer satisfaction.

In conclusion, financial management is a critical component of effective management. Managers who understand financial statements, performance metrics, and budgeting and forecasting can make informed decisions that benefit the organization and its stakeholders. By managing cash flow, investing wisely, reducing expenses, and measuring ROI, managers can improve the financial health of their organizations and ensure long-term success.

CHAPTER 16: DEVELOPING LEADERSHIP SKILLS

Leadership is a crucial aspect of management that distinguishes great managers from average ones. While some people are born with leadership qualities, anyone can develop and enhance their skills with the right mindset, approach, and practice. In this chapter, we will define leadership, explore different leadership styles, highlight the importance of self-awareness and emotional intelligence, discuss ways to build a leadership brand, and outline how to inspire trust, respect, and influence.

Definition of Leadership

Leadership is the ability to influence and inspire others to achieve a shared vision or goal. It involves setting direction, aligning resources and actions, motivating and supporting individuals and teams, and assessing and adapting to external and internal factors that impact performance and results. Leaders provide guidance and direction, empower others to take ownership and responsibility, and create a positive and productive work environment.

Leadership Styles

Leadership styles refer to the approach, behavior, and mindset that leaders adopt to achieve their goals and interact with others. Different contexts and situations require different leadership styles, and effective leaders can adapt and switch styles as needed. The most common leadership styles include:

- ❖ Autocratic: Leaders who make decisions without consulting others and enforce strict rules and procedures.

- ❖ Democratic: Leaders who involve and empower their team in decision-making and value their input and feedback.

- ❖ Laissez-faire: Leaders who delegate responsibilities and authority to their team and provide minimal guidance or feedback.

- ❖ Transactional: Leaders who reward or punish their team based on their performance and adherence to rules and expectations.

- ❖ Transformational: Leaders who inspire and motivate their team to achieve a shared vision and values and encourage innovation, creativity, and continuous learning.

Self-Awareness and Self-Reflection

Self-awareness and self-reflection are fundamental for effective leadership. They involve understanding one's strengths, weaknesses, values, personality traits, biases, and emotions and their impact on others. Great leaders should invest time and effort to develop their self-awareness and self-reflection skills by seeking feedback from others, conducting regular self-assessments, and continuously learning and growing.

Building a Leadership Brand

A leadership brand refers to the unique set of skills, values, and behaviors that define a leader's identity and reputation. Building a leadership brand requires consistent and intentional effort to align one's actions and words with their vision, values, and goals, and to cultivate a positive and authentic image among colleagues, employees, and stakeholders. Strategies for building a leadership brand include:

❖ Defining and communicating a clear vision, mission, and values

❖ Demonstrating integrity and ethical behavior in all decisions and actions

❖ Inspiring and motivating others through storytelling, recognition, and empowerment

❖ Encouraging diversity, inclusion, and innovation

❖ Seeking and providing regular feedback and coaching

❖ Developing and maintaining strong relationships with stakeholders and peers

❖ Staying current with industry trends and best practices

❖ Leading by example and taking ownership of mistakes and failures

Developing Emotional Intelligence

Emotional intelligence (EI) refers to the ability to recognize, understand, regulate, and express emotions and to use them to navigate social interactions and relationships effectively. EI includes several components, such as self-awareness, self-regulation, empathy, motivation, and social skills. Developing EI can enhance leadership skills by improving communication, conflict resolution, decision-making, and collaboration. Strategies for developing EI include:

❖ Practicing mindfulness and self-reflection

❖ Developing empathy and active listening skills

- ❖ Managing stress and emotions through self-regulation and self-care

- ❖ Building positive relationships and networks

- ❖ Fostering a positive and inclusive work environment

- ❖ Encouraging open communication and feedback

- ❖ Recognizing biases and stereotypes and challenging them

- ❖ Acknowledging and learning from mistakes and failures

Leading with Empathy

Empathy refers to the ability to understand and share the feelings, perspectives, and experiences of others. Empathy is a critical leadership skill that enables leaders to connect and engage with their team, build trust and relationships, and create a supportive and empowering work environment. Leaders who lead with empathy can inspire and motivate their team, recognize and anticipate their needs, and respond to their concerns and feedback effectively. Strategies for leading with empathy include:

- ❖ Active listening and asking open-ended questions

- ❖ Seeking feedback and input from team members

- ❖ Acknowledging and validating emotions and concerns

- ❖ Offering support and assistance when needed

- ❖ Encouraging work-life balance and self-care

- ❖ Recognizing and celebrating achievements and milestones

- ❖ Avoiding blame and criticism and focusing on solutions and opportunities

- ❖ Modeling empathy and providing opportunities for team members to practice empathy

Inspiring Trust and Respect

Trust and respect are essential elements of effective leadership. Leaders who inspire trust and respect can create a loyal, committed, and engaged team, promote collaboration, and produce excellent results. Trust and respect are built through consistent and transparent communication, ethical behavior, leading by example, delivering on commitments, and providing opportunities for growth and development. Strategies for inspiring trust and respect include:

- ❖ Communicating honestly, clearly, and regularly
- ❖ Demonstrating empathy, integrity, and authenticity
- ❖ Treating others with respect and dignity
- ❖ Being consistent and fair in decisions and actions
- ❖ Providing praise, recognition, and feedback
- ❖ Addressing conflicts and concerns openly and constructively
- ❖ Encouraging innovation and creativity
- ❖ Maintaining confidentiality and privacy

Building Influence

Influence refers to the ability to persuade, guide, and impact others' attitudes, behaviors, and actions. Leaders who have influence can create change, mobilize resources, and achieve their goals effectively. Building influence requires a strategic mindset, communication skills, and relationship building. Strategies for building influence include:

- ❖ Developing and communicating a compelling vision and mission

- ❖ Identifying key stakeholders and their interests and needs

- ❖ Finding common ground and building alliances

- ❖ Using storytelling and emotional appeals

- ❖ Providing evidence and data to support arguments

- ❖ Creating a sense of urgency and excitement

- ❖ Building credibility and trust through relationships and performance

- ❖ Continuously learning and improving one's skills and knowledge.

In conclusion, building leadership skills is an ongoing and rewarding journey for managers who aspire to excel and make an impact. Great leaders embody and model the values and behaviors they seek in others, inspire and empower their team, and create a culture of trust, respect, and innovation. By developing self-awareness, emotional intelligence, empathy, and influence, managers can become great leaders and achieve their personal and organizational goals.

CHAPTER 17: NETWORKING AND PROFESSIONAL DEVELOPMENT

Networking and professional development are essential for managers who want to stay ahead in today's fast-paced business world. These activities help to build strong relationships, develop new skills, and stay up-to-date with the latest trends and practices in the industry. In this chapter, you will learn why networking and professional development are crucial for your career success and how you can get started.

Importance of Networking

Building professional relationships can provide many benefits for business managers. Networking allows you to:

❖ Connect with other professionals in your industry: Networking will help you meet other professionals in your field with whom you can share experiences, challenges, and knowledge. Through these relationships, you can gain new ideas and insights into your industry.

❖ Increase your visibility: Attending industry events and building relationships with people in your industry can help you increase your visibility. This exposure can help you become more known in your field and create opportunities for your career growth.

❖ Develop new business opportunities: Networking can help you discover new business opportunities that may not have been available without the connections you have made.

❖ Gain referrals and recommendations: Building relationships with people in your industry can lead to referrals and recommendations from others who are familiar with your work and your personal brand.

Building Professional Relationships

The key to networking is building and maintaining strong relationships. Here are some ways in which you can build meaningful connections in your industry:

❖ Join industry groups: Joining industry groups is one way to meet professionals in your field. Consider joining online groups, social networks, and industry associations that align with your interests and career goals.

❖ Attend industry events: Attend conferences, trade shows, and seminars to meet other professionals in your field.

❖ Volunteer your time: Volunteering for industry-related events and causes is another way to meet people in your field while giving back to your community.

❖ Reach out to others: Reach out to other professionals in your industry through email, social media, or other communication channels. Be respectful and courteous in your approach.

❖ Participate in online forums: Participating in online forums and communities related to your industry is a great way to connect with other professionals in your industry.

❖ Invite others to meet: If you've made connections through online communities, forums, or social media, consider inviting people to meet in person over a cup of coffee. This can help solidify a relationship and create opportunities for future collaborations.

Finding a Mentor

Seeking out a mentor is another way to build relationships and expand your professional network. Mentors can provide advice, guidance, and support as you navigate your career path. Look for someone with whom you share common interests, values, and goals. Consider seeking out mentors in your current organization or industry; you can also look for mentors through industry organizations or online communities.

Professional Development

Continuously developing and improving your skills is essential for success as a business manager. Here are some steps you can take to develop your professional skills:

❖ Attend workshops and seminars: Attend workshops and seminars to learn about new trends, techniques, and best practices in your industry. This can help you stay up-to-date on the latest developments in your field.

❖ Take courses and classes: Taking courses and classes is an excellent way to gain new skills and knowledge in your field. Consider enrolling in a professional development program or a master's degree program in business.

❖ Read industry publications and books: Keep up with industry publications and books to stay informed about new trends and changes in your industry.

❖ Participate in online courses: Online courses and webinars are an excellent way to learn from experts in your field.

Consider enrolling in online courses that align with your interests and career goals.

Creating a Personal Brand

Creating a personal brand can help you build a positive reputation and gain recognition for your work. A personal brand allows you to establish yourself as an expert in your field and build trust with your audience. Here are some tips for creating a personal brand:

- ❖ Identify your strengths and expertise: Identify the strengths and expertise that set you apart from others in your field.

- ❖ Determine your values and mission: Determine your personal values and mission and use them to guide your work.

- ❖ Create a strong professional image: Create a professional image by using consistent branding across all your communications. This includes your website, social media, and business cards.

- ❖ Develop a personal narrative: Develop a personal narrative that tells your story and highlights your achievements.

- ❖ Promote your brand: Promote your brand by sharing your expertise and insights with others in your industry. This can be done through blog posts, social media, speaker engagements, or by offering free resources.

Conclusion

Networking and professional development are essential for business managers who want to stay ahead in today's competitive business world. Building relationships with other professionals in your industry can provide many benefits, including gaining new ideas and insights, visibility, new business opportunities, and referrals. Developing new skills, staying up-to-date with industry trends, and establishing a personal brand can help you become known as an expert in your field, build trust with your audience, and create opportunities for professional growth.

CHAPTER 18: MANAGING REMOTE TEAMS

Overview of remote work

Remote work has become an increasingly popular way of working for many organizations, especially in the wake of the COVID-19 pandemic. The internet and the advancements in technology have made it easier for people to work together from different locations and still achieve the same level of productivity. Managing remote teams, however, requires a different set of skills than managing teams that are physically present in an office.

Benefits and challenges of remote work

Remote work has several benefits, such as increased flexibility, improved work-life balance, and reduced commute time and expenses. However, managing remote teams presents a unique set of challenges. One of the primary challenges is ensuring that remote team members feel connected to the team and the organization. Communication can also become an issue due to time zone differences and a lack of face-to-face interaction. Additionally, there is the challenge of managing productivity and ensuring that remote workers are focused and meeting their targets.

Communicating effectively with remote teams

One of the critical tasks of managing a remote team is ensuring open and clear communication channels. Managers need to use different communication tools to communicate with remote team members effectively. Tools like video conferencing, chat tools, email, and project management tools can help keep everyone connected despite the physical distance. Managers should also set clear communication standards and expectations, such as response times, frequency of meetings, and communication protocols.

Creating virtual team culture

A cohesive team is essential in achieving objectives and goals. Remote teams need a strong sense of team culture to work together effectively. Managers should create opportunities for team members to bond, such as virtual coffee breaks, team-building activities, and social events. Celebrating team milestones and accomplishments can also help to improve the team's morale and create a sense of unity.

Providing remote team members with necessary tools and resources

Remote workers require the right tools and resources to be productive. This includes laptops, internet connectivity, and access to software and hardware that are necessary for their roles. Ensuring that remote team members have everything they need to be productive can help prevent delays and frustration.

Virtual collaboration and teamwork

The success of a remote team depends on the ability to collaborate effectively. Managers need to establish clear goals and deadlines for projects and establish protocols for feedback and reviews.

Tools such as project management software, cloud storage, and shared calendars can help keep everyone on the same page. Managers should also encourage collaboration between team members and provide opportunities for them to share ideas and best practices.

Managing performance and productivity

Managing remote teams requires a higher level of trust and accountability. It is essential to set clear expectations for each team member and establish standards for measuring productivity and performance. Managers should monitor output and ensure that their team members are meeting their targets. Providing regular feedback and having performance conversations can help to identify problem areas and find solutions.

Ensuring remote team members feel included

Remote team members may sometimes feel isolated and disconnected from the team. Managers need to ensure that all team members feel included and valued. Keeping team members informed and providing opportunities for virtual interactions can help remote workers feel more connected. Inviting remote team members to events, meetings, and brainstorming sessions can also help them feel like they are part of the team.

Conclusion

Managing remote teams has become a reality for many managers. To be successful, managers need to create a sense of team culture and establish clear communication and expectations. Providing the necessary tools and resources, promoting collaboration and teamwork, and ensuring that remote team members feel included are just a few of the things managers can do to manage remote teams effectively. Managing remote teams requires a different mindset and skill set, but by adopting the right strategies, managers can lead their remote teams to success.

CHAPTER 19: CRISIS MANAGEMENT

No one wants to think about a crisis situation happening at their workplace, but the reality is that it can happen to any organization. Whether it's a natural disaster, a security breach, or a scandal involving the leadership, a crisis can leave a lasting impact on the organization and its employees. As a manager, it's important to be prepared and equipped to handle a crisis, and this chapter will provide the necessary guidance to manage through a difficult time.

Definition of Crisis Management

Crisis management is the process of preparing for, responding to, and recovering from an unexpected event that has the potential to harm an organization's reputation, finances, or operations. A crisis can happen at any time, and it can have a significant impact on the organization and its stakeholders.

Types of Crises

There are several types of crises that an organization may face, including natural disasters, technological failures, legal issues, security breaches, and reputational damage. Natural disasters like hurricanes, floods, and earthquakes can cause physical damage to the workplace and disrupt operations, while technological failures like system crashes or cybersecurity breaches can compromise confidential information and disrupt business operations. Legal issues like lawsuits and regulatory violations can also harm a company's reputation and finances. Reputational damage can occur due to a crisis involving company leadership or employees, a product recall, or negative media coverage.

Preparing for a Crisis

While no one can predict when a crisis will happen, it's important for managers to be prepared in case one does occur. This involves developing a crisis management plan that outlines the roles and responsibilities of key personnel, communication protocols, and steps for recovery. The plan should also be regularly tested and evaluated to ensure its effectiveness in real-life scenarios.

Developing a Crisis Management Plan

When developing a crisis management plan, it's important to identify potential crises that the organization may face, and determine the most effective way to respond to each. The plan should also include contact information for key personnel who will be responsible for managing the crisis, including the CEO, legal counsel, HR, and public relations.

Communication During a Crisis

Effective communication is critical during a crisis, and the crisis management plan should outline the steps for communicating with internal and external stakeholders. This includes employees, customers, vendors, media, and regulatory agencies. The communication should be timely, accurate, and transparent, while also conveying empathy and concern for those affected by the crisis.

Managing the Aftermath of a Crisis

Once the initial crisis has been handled, it's important to assess the impact of the crisis on the organization and determine the steps for recovery. This may include rebuilding damaged facilities, repairing relationships with stakeholders, and implementing improvements to prevent similar crises from occurring in the future.

Learning from the Crisis

Finally, it's important for managers to review and evaluate the crisis management plan to determine what worked well and what could be improved upon. This will help ensure that the organization is better prepared for future crises.

Building Resilience

The experience of managing through a crisis can be overwhelming, but it can also be an opportunity to learn and grow. Managers should encourage their teams to embrace the challenges of the crisis and learn from the experience, which can help build resilience and strengthen the organization's ability to handle future challenges.

Conclusion

While no organization wants to experience a crisis, being prepared and having a plan in place can make all the difference in managing the crisis effectively. As a manager, it's important to be proactive in developing a crisis management plan, communicating effectively with stakeholders, and learning from the crisis to improve processes and prevent future crises.

CHAPTER 20: CONCLUSION AND TAKING ACTION

Congratulations! You've made it to the end of this book on how to be a great manager. By now, you should have a better understanding of what it means to be an effective manager and what key skills and traits are needed to succeed in this role.

This chapter is all about taking action. It's time to reflect on what you've learned and start implementing strategies to improve your management performance.

Recap of Key Points:

Throughout this book, we've covered a wide range of topics related to management. We've examined the importance of effective communication, building and leading teams, managing change, setting goals and objectives, managing time and priorities, problem-solving and decision-making, managing performance, motivating employees, negotiation skills, ethical and legal considerations, managing diversity, managing performance and stress, financial management, developing leadership skills, networking and professional development, managing remote teams, and crisis management.

As a great manager, you need to not only master each of these topics but also integrate them all into your management style.

Assessing Your Strengths and Weaknesses:

Now it's time to assess your strengths and weaknesses in each of these areas. Think about where you excel and where you may need to improve. Do you communicate effectively with your team? Are you able to motivate employees to reach their full potential? Are you able to make decisions and solve problems efficiently? Identify your areas of strength and areas that could use improvement.

Setting Personal Goals:

Based on your self-reflection, set personal goals that will help you develop skills in areas where you may be lacking. Use the SMART goal-setting method that we discussed earlier in Chapter 6. Set specific goals with measurable objectives and realistic timelines.

Creating an Action Plan:

Once you've set your personal goals, create an action plan to achieve them. Break down your goals into smaller, more manageable steps, and prioritize them based on what needs to be accomplished first. Remember to be flexible, and adjust your plan as needed.

Building Support Systems:

To achieve your goals, you need a support system. This could include a mentor, a coach, or a colleague in a similar management role. Seek out someone who can provide guidance and advice and who can hold you accountable for achieving your goals. Build relationships with team members, as they can also provide support when needed.

Continuously Learning and Growing:

As a manager, your learning never stops. Attend training sessions, conferences, and workshops to improve your management skills. Read books and articles on management, listen to podcasts and attend webinars. Engage with other professionals in your field to stay current and to continue to learn and grow.

Celebrating Progress:

As you reach milestones in achieving your goals, take time to celebrate your progress. Share your success with your team and reflect on what you've learned along the way. Celebrating progress helps to motivate you to continue to work towards your goals.

Moving Forward with Confidence:

Remember, becoming a great manager takes time, effort, and a willingness to learn and grow. Always aim to improve, and don't be afraid to take risks. As long as you stay grounded in strong and ethical leadership principles, you should continue to move forward with confidence and become the best manager that you can be.

In Conclusion, as a manager, you have a significant impact on your team's success and the organization's overall success. It's essential to cultivate the necessary skills and traits that will help you become a great manager. This book has provided you with a framework to assess your skills and identify areas for growth. By taking action and implementing strategies for improvement, you will be on your way to becoming a great manager that your team will admire, respect, and follow.

Good luck on your journey!

ABOUT THE AUTHOR

Ray Goodwin

Ray Goodwin, is the author behind this series of captivating books on Business Development and self improvement, and has left an indelible mark on the field. He was born and raised in the bustling city of London, where he developed a strong work ethic and an insatiable curiosity about the inner workings of successful businesses. Throughout his illustrious career, Ray leveraged his extensive knowledge and experience to help numerous companies flourish and prosper.

His keen insights and innovative strategies has earned him recognition, driving him to share his expertise with others. Ray believes in the power of sharing knowledge to elevate businesses and empower aspiring entrepreneurs.

Ray's dedication to his craft is evident in the numerous books he has authored on business development and self improvement. His writing style seamlessly blends practical advice, thought-provoking concepts, and real-life case studies, making his books invaluable resources for business professionals and novices alike. His ability to distill complex concepts into accessible language has greatly impacted the lives and careers of countless individuals.

Now retired from the corporate world, Ray and his beloved wife have settled in the idyllic English countryside. Surrounded by the beauty of nature, Ray finds inspiration for his writing and indulges in his hobbies.

Ray Goodwin's books continue to serve as enduring guides for those seeking success in the business world. With a wealth of experience and a deep understanding of the inner workings of businesses, Ray's work remains a testament to his passion for sharing knowledge and helping others flourish.